DEISENSUS
LEADERSHIP

STUDY GUIDE

For foreign and subsidiary rights, contact the author.

Cover design by Sara Young
Cover photo by Andrew van Tilborgh

ISBN 978-1-957369-69-3   1 2 3 4 5 6 7 8 9 10

Printed in the United States of America

LEADING
WITH GOD
IN MIND

DEISENSUS
LEADERSHIP

Dr. Ron Crum

STUDY GUIDE

AVAIL

CONTENTS

LEADING
WITH GOD
IN MIND

DEISENSUS LEADERSHIP

Dr. Ron Crum

SUDDEN SHIFTS: THE DYNAMICS OF EVER-CHANGING LEADERSHIP

The voice of God emerges from
the collective voice of the team
God has placed around you.

READING TIME

As you read Chapter 1: "Sudden Shifts" in *Deisensus Leadership*, review, reflect on, and respond to the text by answering the following questions.

REVIEW, REFLECT, AND RESPOND:

When have you experienced a sudden shift in your leadership role that demanded more of you? How do you respond to unexpected pivots?

_____

_____

_____

_____

_____

_____

_____

_____

_____

_____

_____

How did others respond to the changes you had to make to accommodate that shift?

_____

_____

_____

_____

_____

_____

_____

_____

_____

_____

_____

Have you ever had to adapt to changing dynamics in your organization after moving under new leadership?

_____

_____

_____

_____

_____

_____

Review the six leadership issues addressed at the end of this chapter. What stood out to you about each one? Did you notice the areas in which your organization may need more support?

_____

_____

_____

_____

_____

_____

What is your organization's approach to creating a healthy environment of authority?

_____

_____

_____

_____

_____

_____

How empowered are the people working alongside you to weigh in on important matters in crisis scenarios?

_____

_____

_____

_____

_____

_____

Where do you see or have you seen authoritarian leadership, either in your own organization or another? How well did the organization function and respond to crisis?

_____

_____

_____

_____

_____

_____

In your organization, what role does each team or board member play in decision-making processes? How "in the know" are they?

_____

_____

_____

_____

_____

_____

In what ways can you relate to the tendency to "satisfice" when the pressure of a high-demand situation arises?

_____

_____

_____

_____

_____

_____

What level of responsibility do you give the Holy Spirit to guide you and your team to reach ethical, reasonable, and responsible decisions?

_____

_____

_____

_____

_____

_____

How does a top-down culture restrict or stifle efforts to lead effectively?

_____

_____

_____

_____

_____

_____

Consider whether your organization practices centralized or de-centralized funding. Where do you find the leading of the Holy Spirit in your practices?

_____

_____

_____

_____

_____

_____

_____

What does it mean to put people first during a transition? How well does your organization put the "people first" mentality into action?

_____

_____

_____

_____

_____

_____

_____

Taken from Acts 15:28, consider the phrase "it seemed good to the Holy Spirit and us." How do you apply this Scripture daily to an ever-changing organization?

_____

_____

_____

_____

_____

_____

_____

DEISENSUS
DISCOVERED

If you lead very long, you will find that the very best decisions can go off the rails, and you wonder how you missed it. Our best is simply never enough: we need God's help.

READING TIME

As you read Chapter 2: *"Deisensus Discovered"* in *Deisensus Leadership*, review, reflect on, and respond to the text by answering the following questions.

REVIEW, REFLECT, AND RESPOND:

In your own words, what does a *Deisensus* (Spirit-led) decision-making approach entail? How do you understand it as it applies to leadership making decisions?

_____

_____

_____

_____

_____

_____

_____

_____

_____

Identify a time when you relied on your own intellect or path of human reasoning to arrive at an important decision. Looking back, how could you have elevated God into the position of decision-maker?

_____

_____

_____

_____

_____

_____

_____

_____

_____

Using Acts 15:28 as an example, how is Holy Spirit-led leadership drastically different than man-made leadership?

_____

_____

_____

_____

_____

_____

What parallels can you draw between the transition from man-led decision-making to Spirit-led decision-making and salvation by circumcision to salvation by grace?

_____

_____

_____

_____

_____

_____

When have you adopted a *Deisensus* model of decision-making and what kind of fruit did it bear in accomplishing initiatives and deepening relationships within your organization?

_____

_____

_____

_____

_____

_____

Where did you see the surrender to the Holy Spirit and His leading in the West Virginia miracle?

_____

_____

_____

_____

_____

_____

_____

Where do *Deisensus* leadership and inviting others into the leadership process intersect?

_____

_____

_____

_____

_____

_____

_____

What does the author's story about the renovation costs he faced in building the new church tell you about the Spirit's superior timing to our own?

_____

_____

_____

_____

_____

_____

_____

Refer to the story of the financial officer who resigned due to financial dishonesty. What might have happened if the impressions of the Holy Spirit had *not* been heeded?

_____

_____

_____

_____

_____

_____

_____

_____

_____

Consider a time when you noticed excessive praise was being given to a leader. In what ways did shifting the attention away from the Holy Spirit impact the leader, the people under his leadership, and the organization as a whole?

_____

_____

_____

_____

_____

_____

_____

_____

_____

_____

What differences have you noticed between an organization that leans collectively on the Holy Spirit and one that draws on its own strength to make decisions?

_____

_____

_____

_____

_____

_____

_____

_____

_____

LEADING
WITH GOD
IN MIND

DEISENSUS VS. THE FOUR-WAY PATH TO DECISION-MAKING

Deisensus says that beyond what we may want, beyond what the felt need may be, and beyond what may be best at this moment, we are deeply committed to following the leading of the Holy Spirit and pleasing Him.

READING TIME

As you read Chapter 3: *"Deisensus vs. the Four-Way Path to Decision-Making"* in *Deisensus Leadership*, review, reflect on, and respond to the text by answering the following questions.

REVIEW, REFLECT, AND RESPOND:

The author advocates for making Spirit-led decision-making your dominant path for leading. What is your "default" mode when faced with important decisions? What about your team?

_____

_____

_____

_____

_____

_____

_____

_____

_____

_____

What kind of discrepancies in decision-making styles have you found between your team members? What steps can you take to get on the same page?

_____

_____

_____

_____

_____

_____

_____

_____

_____

When you think of what it means to be successful as a leader of your organization, what comes to mind? What could you add or subtract from that to align with what God says about success?

_____

_____

_____

_____

_____

_____

Refer to the four ways leaders make decisions (authoritarian, democratic, consensus, laissez-faire). Which most closely corresponds to the way you make decisions? Which deviates most from your decision-making approach?

_____

_____

_____

_____

_____

_____

Review and answer the following questions about the five decision-making styles.

AUTHORITARIAN DECISION-MAKING

Identify a time when you witnessed the authoritarian model of leadership work well in your or someone else's organization. How did that specific context lend itself well to the authoritarian model?

_____

_____

_____

_____

_____

_____

_____

When an urgent matter requires an authoritarian leadership approach, who outside of your organization could you consult to maximize effectiveness for making critical decisions?

_____

_____

_____

_____

_____

_____

_____

How do you think a team typically responds to an authoritarian leader? Where does the authoritarian style of leadership fall apart? Provide an example from your own life.

_____

_____

_____

_____

_____

_____

_____

_____

DEMOCRATIC DECISION-MAKING

At first blush, what about the aspects of a democratic model sound good?

_____

_____

_____

_____

_____

_____

Consult the Tannenbaum and Schmidt Continuum of Leadership Behavior diagram. What stands out to you about this model of decision-making? Where do you see drawbacks, and where do you see strengths?

_____

_____

_____

_____

_____

_____

In what ways might a democratic model dilute or confuse the path to reaching a good decision?

_____

_____

_____

_____

_____

CONSENSUS DECISION-MAKING

How do you understand the differences between the democratic and consensus decision-making models?

_____

_____

_____

_____

_____

_____

_____

What is your initial response to the concept of vigilance as a necessary component of the consensus model? Does it appeal to you? Does it feel fatiguing? How so?

_____

_____

_____

_____

_____

_____

_____

What about the consensus model conflicts with the full utilization of the Holy Spirit in the decision-making process?

_____

_____

_____

_____

_____

_____

_____

LAISSEZ-FAIRE DECISION-MAKING

Considering delegation as the heart of laissez-faire decision-making, how would you effectively approach delegation? What does inappropriate or ineffective execution of delegation look like?

_____

_____

_____

_____

_____

_____

_____

What is your overall assessment of a laissez-faire decision-making approach?

_____

_____

_____

_____

_____

_____

_____

Have you ever felt the process of decision-making going nowhere? How might have misguided delegation played a role?

_____

_____

_____

_____

_____

_____

DEISENSUS DECISION-MAKING

How does Appreciative Inquiry intersect with the *Deisensus* approach to decision-making?

_____

_____

_____

_____

_____

_____

_____

_____

_____

Review the contrasts the author makes between the *Deisensus* model and the other four models. In what ways does adopting the *Deisensus* model resolve the flaws and consequences that often come with the others?

_____

_____

_____

_____

_____

_____

_____

_____

_____

_____

_____

DEISENSUS
IN ACTION

Holy Spirit-led decision-making, regardless
of a leader's decision-making and leadership
style, intentionally seeks God's will—nothing
more, nothing less, nothing else.

READING TIME

As you read Chapter 4: *"Deisensus in Action"* in *Deisensus Leadership*, review, reflect on, and respond to the text by answering the following questions.

REVIEW, REFLECT, AND RESPOND:

Prior to reading this chapter, had you considered the biblical model of decision-making? How would you have explained it?

_____

_____

_____

_____

_____

_____

_____

_____

How does the journey through the Old Testament to the New Testament demonstrate the influence of deeply ingrained traditions on new opportunities and changing cultural mandates?

_____

_____

_____

_____

_____

_____

_____

_____

What parallels have you observed between the biblical narrative of man-led versus Spirit-led decision-making and decision-making among leaders in the marketplace and in the Church?

_____

_____

_____

_____

_____

_____

What can you learn from the Bible about navigating the challenge of opposing voices when arriving at an important decision?

_____

_____

_____

_____

_____

_____

Carefully consider Peter's speech and James' address to the council and refer back to the five most common approaches to decision-making outlined in Chapter 2. How did their approach to reaching consensus differ from the first four approaches (authoritarian, democratic, consensus, and laissez-faire)?

_____

_____

_____

_____

_____

_____

How did James' presentation of the Noahide precepts work to unite Jews and Gentiles rather than divide them? What purpose did they play in the effort to embody Spirit-led decisions?

_____

_____

_____

_____

_____

_____

One of the many functions of James' letter was to correct and rebuke the leaders of the Jerusalem church for misleading the people of Antioch. How is this aspect of leadership addressed in a *Deisensus* decision-making model?

_____

_____

_____

_____

_____

_____

How could the united leadership of Paul and the other leaders apply to Spirit-led decision-making in your own organization?

_____

_____

_____

_____

_____

_____

What needs to happen on your team in order to mimic the leadership dynamics between Paul and the other leaders?

_____

_____

_____

_____

_____

_____

What can you learn from Luke's successful efforts in uniting members of the Church with a diverse set of values and personal interests? How do you reach decisions when you are working with diverse needs, preferences, and personalities?

_____

_____

_____

_____

_____

_____

In your own words, describe the evolution of reaching a consensus among the Jewish leaders on the necessity of Gentile circumcision for salvation and full fellowship rights. Pay special attention to the way the New Testament leaders' stories intersected, conflicted, and converged to ultimately arrive at a Holy Spirit-empowered decision.

_____

_____

_____

_____

_____

_____

_____

_____

Why is Holy Spirit-led decision-making the only option for a leader?

_____

_____

_____

_____

_____

_____

_____

_____

LEADING
WITH GOD
IN MIND

POSITIONING TO HEAR FROM GOD

Decision-makers who believe in their own
perfect rationality—the thinking that their
style, method, process, procedure, or rules
produce the only possible choice— block their
own access to information and options.

READING TIME

As you read Chapter 5: "Positioning to Hear from God" in *Deisensus Leadership*, review, reflect on, and respond to the text by answering the following questions.

REVIEW, REFLECT, AND RESPOND:

Reflect on a time when you reached a decision based on the notion of perfect rationality. What led you to rely on this style of decision-making? Looking back, what other options may have been available to you that you didn't consider?

_____

_____

_____

_____

_____

_____

_____

_____

When have you taken a maximizer approach to decision-making? What was the outcome? What worked well? Were there any costs accrued from this approach?

_____

_____

_____

_____

_____

_____

_____

_____

_____

Where did you see *Deisensus* leadership represented in the author's search for an employee to oversee the new hires?

_____

_____

_____

_____

_____

_____

_____

Define Appreciative Inquiry in your own words. Where have you seen Appreciative Inquiry in action?

_____

_____

_____

_____

_____

_____

Consider the Appreciative Inquiry 4-D cycle of discovery, dream, design, and destiny. Choose one area you would like to mobilize in your organization. How does this model provide a cohesive and comprehensive framework for bringing it to life?

_____

_____

_____

_____

_____

_____

What about capitalizing on the strengths of a leader or organization produces forward momentum in the desired direction? Why does a limitations-based approach tend to work against leaders looking to grow and flourish?

_____

_____

_____

_____

_____

_____

_____

Refer to the three questions Appreciative Inquiry poses and collaborate with your team to answer those questions.

_____

_____

_____

_____

_____

_____

_____

Write down your organization's top five weaknesses. Rewrite them as a proposal for what is possible. How do these new possibilities lay a healthy foundation on which to cultivate a culture of Spirit-led decision-making?

_____

_____

_____

_____

_____

_____

Why is discerning the will of God in an organizational setting a collective exercise and not an individual one?

_____

_____

_____

_____

_____

_____

_____

To what extent is discerning the will of God before moving on a decision a priority in your organization?

_____

_____

_____

_____

_____

_____

_____

How congruent is your answer to the model of joint discernment outlined in this chapter? What are the missing pieces that your team needs to follow this model more closely?

_____

_____

_____

_____

_____

_____

_____

What practical steps can you take to, alongside your team, spiritually prepare for discerning the will of God in making important decisions?

_____

_____

_____

_____

_____

_____

_____

_____

_____

_____

_____

LEADING
WITH GOD
IN MIND

.

Printed in the USA
CPSIA information can be obtained
at www.ICGtesting.com
JSHW011802080524
62739JS00003B/19